All about Love

ISBN 976-8077-808

Preface

What is it that makes you tick?
Love
What is it that makes me click?
Same as above

People have varying experiences with love. An experience
of love that makes one person happy can simultaneously
make another sad.

Love has many angles. In my book I seek to look at love from
the perspective of both sexes. I also try to make the poems as
real as possible.

When reading you might make comments like "That can't
happen", "That is him he is talking about" or " I know
someone to whom this has happened". Comments like those
will make me know I have succeeded in getting my humour
and at times serious messages across in a practical and real
life manner.

I hope you enjoy the book. Remember Love is
not a toy, use love to spread joy.

Love,

Bing Bong

Words associated with Love

Tick	Beat	Vex
Stick	Cheat	_ _x
Slick	Weak	Wet
Kick	Feet	Fret
Trick	Meat	Forget

Gifts for Loved ones

Car	Flowers	Perfume
Hug	Kiss	Stupidness
Squeeze	Wine	Chocolates

Persons to Love

Brother	Aunt	Sister
Mother	Honey	Father
Wife	Son	Sweetheart
	Daughter	

Something that shouldn't buy Love

"Money"

Contents...

... Contents

The Hibiscus in awesome beauty brings love thoughts to the fore

One morning, I woke up early
And looked through my window
There; a Hibiscus in awesome beauty
Made love thoughts just start to flow

In the background were some clouds
Fluffy, white and truly pretty
The red against the white said love
I thought of when people marry

Later in the day, the clouds turned gray
That same Hibiscus stood there
Pitted now against those darkened clouds
The message a different kind of love

I began to think of relationships
Abysmal, lost on the verge of quits
One in which one partner no longer cares
And the other hoping those clouds would clear

The clouds of love may darken further
Soon sunset will see them disappear
But another day will be tomorrow
And the Hibiscus will still be there

Wake up therefore to reality
Looking forward to fluffy white clouds
The Hibiscus the symbol of love and beauty
Will start your day with feelings of LOVE

Baby's Here

Oopps! I popped out
A small passage was my route
Shut up your mouth
You loud mouth boy
Mother's face, a bundle of joy

Inside I had nothing to fear
Not a bath for 'bout a year
Only two minutes of fresh air
And hear what nursie say
"Bathe that boy you just brought here"

Comments they made I understood
Some of course were not too good
This one came from my daddy
Are you sure he's the right baby?
If only I could bite he

Then there's Language Magic
Silent words babies interpret
Vividly I remember auntie's visit
In her mind I looked half sick
Badly I felt, I must admit

Uncle Tom and I were friends
'Twas like that until his end
With gestation over. I remember
He predicted my future
"Boy you'll be a great author"

Mother don't think I've forgotten you
With you the words of love ring through
You are special , you are sweet
It's you who gave me food to eat,
Long before "your boy" had teet'

Getting old I'm half way there
So glad I am you brought me here
Thirteen of October it is a fact
You and Daddy got in the act
How I know that ? I traced back

Love For Christmas

Christmas does be crazy
  People adore it
    Shopping in a frenzy
      They buy loads of 'spit'

      Last Christmas a madman
    Cut off his woman's hand
  You should hear the man in court
She wouldn't give me pork

Dad when you get pay
Said this little boy
Buy me a negligé
Forget about the toy

A smart lady wanted money
And saw some expensive art
She went and showed her honey
Said she "Can you give me part?"

Merchants they love Christmas
  They rake in big profits
    Commercialism so ridiculous
      I refuse to be part of it

My Family

I love my car
I love my house
I love coffee and tea

All that love is puny
When I consider my family

I will share my car
I will share my house
I will share coffee and tea

But no one can get me
To share my love for my family

Love for family must manifest
Itself, not only in words
I wash her dress, then I press
To lighten up her load

I romp in bed with my children
When I come home from work
My darling Homo sapiens
With me they go to church

My family is so special
We kneel with mum and pray
To us God is so wonderful
We give thanks everyday

A Child's Love

She was no fool
But hated school
So why she came?

Her bulging eyes
Would open wide
Whenever he came

She would quickly run
Grab bag and books
Put hands around his 'bum'

Repeating this act
Every morning at school
She was her teacher's mule

Learning was fun
When he was around
To others she never listened

Then one day
Sally took up a pen
A love letter she wrote to him

The paper was white
The ink was red
This is what she said

Forgive me if I'm wrong
But for too long
I wanted to tell you this

Every night before
I hit my bed
I would blow you a kiss

I would watch it go
Through the door
And land upon your lips

Quietly I would lie
Upon my back
Hoping you'd send one back

The teacher smiled
He called the child
With her he had a chat

In an adult's world
You are my girl
Wait! There'll be time for that

With sunken head
And mumbling word
She said "Better off dead"

Ungrateful Love

Two women in a conversation
Was something you should hear
With their relationships over and done
They had nothing good to say

Johnny came home late from work
Jump straight into my bed
The smell coming from his shirt
Was enough to kill you dead

If you hear how Johnny snore
Especially on his back
All the neighbours from next door
Would call and ask "What's that?"

Harry ate everything in sight
And went off to sleep
Then in the middle of the night
He tells me he wants to eat

One night as Harry slept
He missed and shout out Jane
I confronted the hypocrite
Said he, "Isn't that your middle name?"

I'll never forget last Valentine's
We went to the sea that day
That 'funny-funny' man of mine
Bathe in my underwear

My Harry he lied too much
Said he was 'loaded' at the bank
His book I never saw or touch
'Til he left it in his pants

I was looking for five digits
But what a surprise I got
The account was in deficit
I am still in shock

They kept on telling their stories
Nothing was pleasing to my ear
Thought it would be temporary
But sixty women gathered there

In disgust I walked on straight
The hate I couldn't take
I then pondered whether men could
Ever be appreciated for their good

Boy Days

Things that happen to boys in love
Are enough to drive you mad
My first experience was in a tub
The best I have ever had

Just seeing her made electricity
Through my body flow
Put a light bulb on me
And be sure to see it glow

Popping a kiss when we meet
Was inevitable
So I always scrub my teeth
To make her comfortable

At times I lacked good sense
Always wanting to impress
One birthday out of ignorance
I gave her my mother's dress

I used to hear about wet dreams
One night I got up wet
I called, asked her what it means
She said it must be sweat

Now I look in retrospect
Boys them days were wild
Without any disrespect
Two men fathered one child

A True Friend

Tall and pretty, a beauty
She's my best friend's lady
Rice and peas with steamed salt fish
She cooks the best Caribbean dish

She was the envy of the neighbourhood
Men would say, "If only I could"
Dignified and full of pride
She denied the ones who tried

Then one day as I passed by
She smiled, then winked a sweet eye
Can I do that to my friend?
Was the question I kept asking

I know at times the flesh is weak
And urges can drive one to cheat
But it takes two to do a do
I won't be tempted to eat that food

Her husband a man I respect
Experiences we share I never forget
I can't do that to my best friend
That would be the gravest sin

So when her advances kept coming
I put her straight; I did offend
But in the end he was my friend
So I stood firm unlike most men

Your Eyes

I pretended I couldn't see
How your eyes walked up and down on me
Out of the corner you took a look
Something told me to stay put

Rolling around just like a ball
The white in them made a call
I got up and ventured near
I thought you had something to say

To my surprise you didn't respond
My whole being felt so down
Just as I heaved one sigh
I realised you were crossed eyed

The Hibiscus a symbol of love and beauty starts your day with feelings of LOVE

Two Hundred Percent

One hundred percent each must give
Fifty, fifty destroys marriage
When you get vexed and feel incensed
I'll still be giving one hundred percent

If you complain 'bout having to cook,
Easy recipes are in cook books.
My hundred percent I'll put in a dish
Sure to smile when you finish.

I won't be like a friend of mine
He tricked his wife several times
Half his salary went to the bank
Still he gave one hundred percent

Two hundred percent will make it work,
It will cover us when somebody shirks.
Commitment to this theory of mine
Means our marriage won't reach ninety nine

The C's of a Marriage

Communication: It's the cornerstone, the foundation
Without it marriages break down

Co-operation: If you don't co-operate
Both will separate

Commitment: Commitment partners trust
Don't be side-tracked by lust

Cohesion: The love must stick like glue
Not only when it's new

Care: You must care today
Like you did yesterday

Confidence: The lack of it is ignorance

Copulation:
&   When you copulate...
Children: Children you create

Christ: He's the pillar on which to stand
Put any problem in his hand

Church: Marriage is built upon the Church
Take time out to do God's work

Open your 👁 👁 and "C".

Why Get Married

The wedding was fun
Reception was great
Men folk drank nuff rum
Ate and congregate

Mark in disconnected words
Made me feel sorry for he
Said he got marry because
  He wife's family had money

  Roger was a tiger
   Who use to chase 'nuff' cat
    His wife said you better
      Marry me, or let me scratch

    Ronald's wife wore short dress
    Reaching above her knees
    He was caught up with flesh
His woman was a tease

But why do men get marry
Asked a sober one in the bunch
He got married to his Susie
  Because she brought him lunch

  For me personally
    She threatened to leave
      In hell I was completely
      Nothing made her please

    People marry for different reasons
    Some for more others for less
    But longevity of unions
  Is the acid test

Horns

Oh how Tommy used to laugh
When she cheated on her man
He would put his account in overdraft
To satisfy this woman

Listen to him on the telephone
And the questions he would ask
Is that donkey of yours home?
Can I come at last?

No one in the world was like he
So she never protected herself
But if the donkey come by she
Gloves came off the shelf

One day things got messed up
He caught her in the act
Quietly that chapter in his life he shut
Never to look back

Tom moved in took full control
Behind her he dodged and peeped
No trust he placed in that girl
There was the fear of cheat

The more you look the less you see
So he came up with a plan
Up in the ceiling he would be
And wait until the phone rang

That was the worst thing he ever did
Her voice was loud and clear
"He gone overseas," she said
"About what time will you get here?"

His body got too heavy
Or the ceiling strip too weak
As she got everything ready
He fell through and broke both feet

From this a lesson can be learnt
By every single man
Too many times I have been burnt
So I already understand

Blind Date

Hello! Who is it?
It is Frederick
Hello! What do you want?
Can I speak to Juliette?
No Juliette lives here
From where did you get that idea

But your voice sound so sweet
Yours too
I'm talking to you and my heart miss a beat
Mine too

All day I wanted someone to talk to
With you my wish has now come through
You have the voice of a teenager
The more you talk it sounds sweeter

So as the night progressed
They developed an interest
It must have been fate
They organized a date

He went to town, bought a suit
Went to the bank, withdrew some loot
Off he sped in his old new car
The man outshone the morning star

Up the steps he knocked the door
He was smelling 'sweet for so'
It was like he couldn't wait
The lady he met was seventy-eight

"Hold my cane", she said to he
Lock the door with the single key
Instead of in front she sat behind
Then he knew his date was blind

Hold Me

Hold me! I want you
Without you what would I do

Hold me! Squeeze the life out of me
Drive me crazy baby

Hold me! I want your kiss
Wow! What is this?

Hold me! Touch me anywhere
I don't care

Pass you fingers through my hair
Pause and say I love you dear
With you life has been complete
Press your jaw against my cheek

Hold me! Tomorrow can be yesterday
Who cares

As long as you are near
This weekend will be one day

Stick It

When love goes wrong it is foolishness
To behave as if all was bad before
Why should you forget the hugs and kiss
And throw the good out through love's door

What happens sometimes quite unconsciously
You react to please your friends
What you don't know and do not see
Friends only laugh when your good time ends

The ones who encourage you to curse
And the ones whom you try to please
Their sweethearts in their lives come first
They patch up and make up, when aggrieved

You must be like me and my girl
We don't have the perfect relationship
But there is no one in this world
No one; who can get us to call it quits

That's Love

With sweat running down
I asked him what's wrong
His colour turned pale
His body looked frail
Choked with emotions he remarked
"My sweetheart isn't very smart"
One tear drop, two, three then four
She is living with the guy next door

Why did my son have to tell me
The position in which he found mummy

Now I've turned to whiskey and rum
'Cause my food just won't go down

For him I felt some pity
So I went to hear his lady's story
Said she, "He was never any good!
Never stirred my porridge like he should
Tell him a pretty car not all
Not answering the bell was his downfall
And tell him for me; keep his money
It can't buy my brand of honey."

Abusive Love

The perpetrators of abuse of we children
  Seem to go scotch free
   There is always some arrangement
   Between them and victim's family
   They escape the punishment
   Their future secure
   No one cares 'bout the pain
   That poor child endure
   What is disgusting
   The ones in whom you should be trusting
  Are the ones guilty
Especially, when the abuse is sexually

Chorus
  Because children beg for money
        You mustn't abuse the child
  Thrown out and begging for lodging
        You mustn't abuse the child
  Hungry and in need of food
        You mustn't abuse the child

Let any kindness be coming from the heart
Having nothing to do with their private parts
The neighbour giving your daughter a ride
    Keep a watchful eye
Things about daddy not always lies
    Keep a watchful eye
Why not left a tape running
You might capture something
    Keep a watchful eye
And judges don't waste time
  For such heinous crimes
    I beg, castrate their behind

21

A Calypso.

The Lover Next Door

I was in love with the girl next door
In love with her and she didn't know
I couldn't tell her, I was too shy
After all I was just a boy

From my bedroom behind the blind
I peeped and looked so many times
Her window was there right next to mine
The things I saw just blew my mind

One day I caught her doing something
I kept quiet; I said nothing
I rushed out of my room for a closer peep
She was cooking stew but didn't have meat

I eased back home took a piece of meat
Instead of one, now two will eat
The flames glowed everything was proper
You know she forgot to put in water

She couldn't cook I knew for sure
But she was my queen who lived next door
She was the one whom when I felt down
Could lift my spirit from off the ground

Sweet Dreams

It was something I dreamed of
  You in my arms again
    Re-kindled memories once lost
    My emotions flowed like rain

      We rolled over in the bed
        Touched what was out of bounds
          So excited I bumped my head
        And fell onto the ground

      All those things we did before
      Was a joy to start again
      She pedi and I manicure
      We played some teasing games

    On top of the world like an idiot
    At least that's how it seemed
    Imagine the feeling when I woke up
  To realise it was only a dream

Reminiscent Love

You promised never to leave me alone
Still you walked right out of our home
All that was left for me to do
Was reminisce about times spent with you

I remember your broad smile
When I gave birth to your child
I lay in bed, you poked you head
Oh boy! What joy, when you got a boy

You helped to wash the baby's face
The right man in the right place
With you I always felt at ease
Can't understand why you would leave

My son asked, "When will daddy come?"
Mum, "Where is the next meal coming form"
Never thought I would be put through this
Oh how I hate to reminisce

My son will grow, this I know
Things will not always be so
One thing for sure I'll never whore
My Creator provides for even the poor

Poor Fred

Is he dead?
He won't lift his head
Get up; come for food
You know he wouldn't move

Years ago he was not so
He ate and ate food galore
At times more than he need
He was overcome by greed

When I was young he roamed the town
Now all he does is lie down
Pointless extending an invitation
It's hard, but Fred couldn't come

Must I give up
Trying to get him up
I think not
He's still my "soft spot"

Knock! Knock! It's Dr. Ned
I've come to examine Fred
My ears turn red, when he said
"I must pronounce him dead"

Is it Love?

We talk about loving our brother
We talk about wishing him well
But truly; do we love each other?
The answer I can't tell

Start a business and you will see
Exactly what I mean
The hate, the anger, the envy
Too much of it I have seen

My friend bought two taxis
His business lasted two weeks
The poor strugglers just like he
Swept him from off his feet

Strange enough the ones who have
Hardly seek to pull you down
What is true and it is sad
Your own pulls you to the ground

Take the scenario of a ladder
Having six or seven rounds
The ones never wishing you better
Sits on the bottom round

A Kiss

The seed of love is a kiss
That's where true love begins
A few of them I've had to miss
Because of the strangest things

A woman told me of this fellow
Who had orange vanilla teeth
She kissed him and taste butter
I would have put it on his cheek

One of her mates had Pyorrhoea
So she kissed him with mouth closed
Sometimes to make him feel okay
She would squeeze upon his nose

My first kiss, I'll tell you this
I had something strange to eat
The lady's name was Sweet Janice
I swallowed two of her false teeth

She went on to tell of poor Johnny
His breath smelled like an old five cent
She only used to kiss up he
Because he paid her rent

I went and got some mouth wash
Toothbrush, soap and some toothpaste
I thought it time to take a wash
Her 'golf balls'* were landing in my face

* Small balls of spit coming from mouth

Aye...

Oh...oh, Aye..aye
What's that noise I'm hearing?
Oh...oh, Aye...aye
What is it they're doing?

Push...push...aye
It seems like pain galore
I opened the door
Push...push...aye

I took a peep, the noise was deep

It was only when the baby cried
That I knew what was going on inside

Oh...oh, Aye..aye
What's that noise I'm hearing?
Oh...oh, Aye...aye
What is it they're doing?

Aye...cont'd

Push...push...aye
It seems like pain galore
I opened the door
Push...push...aye

I took a peep, the noise was deep

Twenty years later déjà vu
You wouldn't believe, but it's true
Inside that room was somebody
That baby was now the mother to be

The red against the white says love

29

Love for Change

In the midst of laughter, take a pause
Look at life's problems, analyse their cause
I know at times you wine and dine
But do you think of those committing crime

So comfortably you go to sleep
While others wished for food to eat
I've heard you say 'most everyday
If they don't work, they don't get pay

But is there really work out there?
Do certain jobs really pay?
After lunch-money and bus fare
It doesn't worth it, I must declare

Be a lawyer, a doctor is the message you send
We don't teach children to be businessmen
Has anyone ever taught them kitchen-garde
How to begin and then to extend?

Scholarships are given by companies
To exceptional students in their studies
Not one I have heard of for cottage industries
You bound to keep them in poverty

Success sometimes reaches one or two
If you know what they went through
The point I simply want to make
Change the system, it isn't too late

Regret

I used to say some horrible things
  And now I have to pay
    A schizophrenic with lost bearings
      Look at it in that way

      Not a single night goes by
        Without you on my mind
      I must admit I do try
But it is a waste of time

        Once in love always in love
          My friends always say this
        Forgiveness I ask from the above
Whenever I sit and reminisce

Using Jah as my conduit
  With her I communicate
    I've destroyed our relationship
      Now it seems too late

In pain I hang my head in shame
  Still I must live in hope
    If ever I get my girl again
      I have plans to elope.

Granny Don't Worry

Granny don't worry
I will take care of you
When people called me ugly
You taught me what to do

Granny don't worry
I will see you through
I used to feel like somebody
When you prepared my food

Granny don't worry
Somebody I will pay
Digging deep down for money
I'll give for them to care

Granny don't worry
You taught me how to pray
I still laugh at those stories
You read me night and day

So much good you've done for me
Do you think I could leave you there?
Provided there's strength in my body
Granny don't worry I'll care

I'll do It

He loved her so much ; he did
Whatever she wanted he would give

She wanted bananas for her lunch,
In just two days he grew a bunch

She wanted to use the toilet
For her he wanted to do it

To Puerto Rico she wanted a trip
He got a credit card and paid for it

While shopping there she ran out
Of money! That's what I'm talking 'bout
He took a plane and flew back home
To ask his banker for a loan.

She bought this and she bought that
She ate until she got too fat
When she realised the money was gone
Once again she called on Tom.

Golden Girl

She's the prettiest in the world
Her name "Golden Girl"

As an infant she couldn't spell
Slightest thing she cuss like hell

Sexy ears and golden hair
Look at her; pimples appear

Like a banana ripe to eat
She always skinned her yellow teeth
Neighbours treated her with scorn
That was the daily norm

Then one day Mr. Rich passed through
Up the altar she said, "I do"

In awe and in dismay
Ears and eyes opened that day

Subsequently they knocked on her door
She kept feeding the district's poor
Ask her why she's doing so
Says she "I appreciate poor."

Old Man's Love

Old as hell, with silver hair
You want every young girl out there
Better you stick within your league
Spiritual food is what you need

In every party you playing young
Leave that now for your grandson
The day a young girl comes along
Peer pressure will drive her out of town

Imagine walking down the road
And friends humour her in slang
Can you accept or afford
Them laughing at her man

The asset of money, the asset of fame
Helps a little when playing that game
But old man don't be silly
You are of no use with a dead willie

Men like you tried before
All they did was end up poor
For all you men thinking so
I know that's not the way to go

Want Food

I want some
I can't wait
Give me my food
Why hesitate

Hand off me
Love what
You sick
It's only love
When you want it

Excuses, excuses
You always make
Bring something new
There's no headache

ou quarrel and quarrel
When I step next door
But my neighbour
She doesn't behave so

You tell me stop the eating out
I washed my hands, cleaned my mouth
Now I call on you for food
You behaving "screw."

Valentine

Valentine's is flowers
Valentine's is wine
    People make promises
    And break them for Valentine's

Valentine's is going to lunch
Valentine's is about dates
    Calling your girl "honey bunch"
    Is what she appreciates

Valentine's is about lie
Valentine's is rice and meat
    I've seen big men cry
    When their outside woman cheat

Valentine's is having parties
Valentine's is about a kiss
    It is about being lonely
    When there is someone you miss

    I use to love Valentine's
I bought flowers for my dates
That has changed in recent times
'Cause valentines don't reciprocate

My body - My House

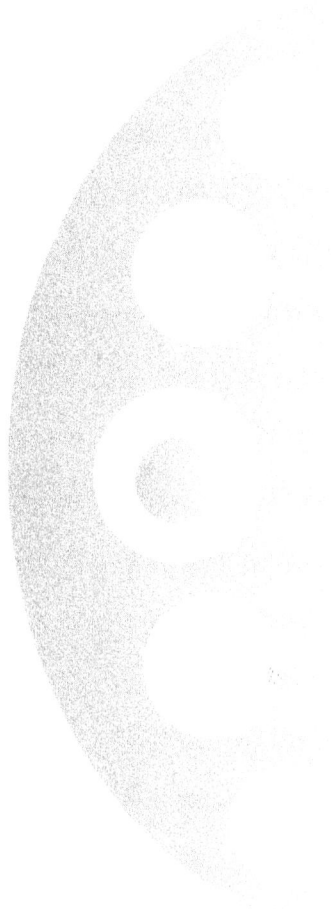

I hold the key
You can't come in
Unless I let you

You can't tell me
What to do,
You are so rude

Men, oh men
Sometimes I hate men
They'll do anything to get in

When they get in
The victory they win
Contempt steps in - A sin

Trust - You want my trust
Give you a chance
....
I guess I must

Careful Love

Life is not only about smiles
So let us pause for a while
Have you given thought to AIDS
The disease that has everyone afraid

I know the value of good health
So I make sure and protect myself
Adolescent behaviour is so weird
At times I wonder if they aren't scared

Everyone has feelings we know that
But that's no excuse for behaving slack
Be smart, get your AIDS test
And of your mate make the same request

I beg my girl don't be promiscuous
The woman lather me with 'cuss'
A good thing I left her right there
It's two years now since she passed away

Imagine a parent with her teenaged 'pride'
Some fellow passes by, flash a smile
Next thing you know emotions run wild
The boy brings AIDS and give your child

So to all concerned, let's get serious
Don't let this disease take its toll on us
Playing around with your life today
Can lead to certain death, O.K.

Reflections

It's time now
Get up and write
Forget the wrongs
Reflect the rights

At the bread shop
Buying bread
Yes it was there
You stole my head
I ran home quick
Called a friend
Your phone number
Came from the other end

Excited I was I must confess
I got the number? Yes!!!
My love for you felt so strong
Stupid me dialed the number wrong

Now I'm old, beginning to gray
I often reflect upon that day
'Twas because of that phone call
I have you, my kids and all.

Since You Are Gone

With you I've tried to make that break
I've looked for someone else to appreciate
I hate to state, it seems my fate
Nothing lasting I can create

The problem has to be with me
This I told myself
Could it be bad breath, my health
Or is it the lack of wealth

The last time I found someone
'Yes' we had a bit of fun
But to tell the truth, I felt used
'Cause every week she wanted shoes

The one before the last...was in a different class
The woman was so fast...half hour didn't past
Tired I relaxed in her bed...Her mother turned red
Hear what she said..."You should be mine instead"

It's ten years now since you've gone
For ten years I've tried to carry on
I never knew I'd miss you like this
Honey your husband was damn foolish

I Love My Man

My man I call him 'Slick Rick'
Yes he makes me tick
   If I don't feel to do something
   I start when I see Rick

   I laugh and laugh yesterday
   'Cause Rick was eating steak
   Over cooked I heard him say
It broke his bottom plate

My man believes in ignorance
He plays mass in mud
Seems like his intelligence
Does him no good

When it comes to cooking
   Of this man I am afraid
   I bought juice and gave him
      He put it in the microwave

For me there is no other
He's as sweet as sweet can be
If I search the world all over
I will still end up with he

Same As You

Says who?
  You can't tell me what to do
    What?
      Mom! My daddy plenty years older than you

      My parents I can't understand,
        They always want to pick my man

        Who says so?
        I want love, I don't care 'bout poor
        What?
        You'll put me at the door

        I love you mummy, you know I do
        But that old man I love him too

        You say he's old and gray
        But he satisfies me okay

      Mummy you better be focus
      These young fellows not serious.

Mother: I guess it's true when I study it
          Forgive me for being inconsiderate
            When I trace my history
              It was the same with your daddy.

Mis'placed Love

Hands off me
Don't touch me there
True Dads don't behave
In that way

When I was small
You push and prod
All I did
Was pray to God

Now I'm old
I now understand
My step-father
Can't be my man

I remember and remember well
You did what you did and said don't tell
You pulled off my dress , and I ingest
I didn't know it was incest
I'm haunted now by those memories
Now I must seek therapy

What must be done to dads like you
Amended laws are now overdue
With all the strength in my body
I'll work to protect abused babies
And governments too have a moral duty
To protect the unborn from these Daddi

In My Bed

What would you do
If in your nest,
You found a man
Taking a rest?

And what if
The one that you love
Is lying right next
To that turtle dove?

I would close the window
Lock the door
Beat him soft
'Till he get off

That's harsh , my good friend said
I would lie down in my bed;
I would urge the two to continue
Try to relax and enjoy the view

Not me ! you must be ignorant
Lying there, I just couldn't
My greatest fear would definitely be
He might leave out her and start on me

I was joking when I said that
Boy I would get a heart attack
And if it didn't take me home
I would consider Gramoxone*

Let me quit thinking 'bout it
The thought just makes me sick
I would probably hide under the bed,
Hoping the pressure won't squeeze my head.

* A poisonous substance

Love is what you see

So I leave this page empty.

Inexperience

Because of your guile
I can't smile
You webbed me into your trap

On the telephone
You called my home
And we would have a chat

I was the sweetest
The greatest and the best
At least you told me that

A seed we sow
We watch it grow
A concentration lapse

My mother pray
I heard her say
That fellow is a rat

Time has passed
It didn't last
Put it to experience I lacked

Thanks for Love

With love you taught me how to write
You put the ideas within my sight
Empty thoughts I would have had on love
If they were not given by the One above

Thank you Jehovah for Your love

Sometimes in the middle of my sleep
I got up to make poems complete
When I thought of being rude
Your love has made me respect you

Thank you Almighty for Your love

With poems completed in a few weeks
People say an admirable feat
To God's credit, I give all praise
Because of his love, I got ideas

Thank you Most High for Your love

Now it's over to the reading public
To show their appreciation of it
If only a few copies are sold
With God's love I've achieved my goal

Thank you Jehovah for Your love

All About Love

John couldn't wait to get on the plane. He had worked for three years without vacation and was looking forward to spending two weeks on the island of Barbados. He had met his dream woman on the internet, and was excited about meeting her.

There was the honk of a horn and a short one-eyed taxi driver inquired if he were Mr. Harris. His reply was yes and with that he grabbed his suitcase and was off.

Checking in was easy. At about eleven o'clock he was on the plane, seated next to an old lady of about seventy-two years.

The lady kept talking and talking from the moment he sat next to her. She wanted to find out his age, if he had a fiancé, if he were married and of course if he were interested in her. She began to tell of romantic escapades with her former husband. In fact she said she was old but not cold. She said that her deceased husband had died because he couldn't handle her; she was too hot for him.

John couldn't get her to stop talking so he asked for an excuse and went to the lavatory.

So relaxed was he, he fell off to sleep. He 'did a number' but never cleaned himself. In fact when he had fallen off to sleep his pants were still down.

John was awakened by a faint voice which said, "Did you check the lavatory?" He jumped up and without thinking, pulled up his pants. His clean trousers instantly took on the appearance of a mat on which a ripe tomato was crushed. The smell was that of rotten eggs.

In a hurry he was out through the door, leaving a smell which required a special scented disinfectant to remove the odour left on his trail.

The air-hostesses and stewards, with hands to their noses quickly exited the aircraft. The pilot, though locked away in the cockpit, was seen descending the steps with his asthma inhaler, gasping for breath.

How John got through immigration and customs, I don't know, but one thing was certain, no taxi driver was taking him to his hotel.

You should have heard the comments made - "That man is a walking toilet. "What was it you were eating?"

With that he went into his suitcase, grabbed a pants and some soap and ran off to the wash-room for gents. The people on the inside ran out. The scene was similar to that of when the crew was forced to disembark the plane earlier.

In a few minutes he emerged from the lavatory smelling like a rose. He jumped into one of the taxis and was off to his hotel at Seaview Road.

He checked in and went to his room. He was soon sleeping. Within an hour someone knocked on the door. Guess who was there?

The old lady whom he had met on the plane. He closed the door and began to pack for home.

50

www.ingramcontent.com/pod-product-compliance
Lightning Source LLC
Chambersburg PA
CBHW060614030426
42337CB00018B/3063